I0453490

43 Poems for People Who Don't Read Poetry

Selected and with an introduction by the editors of *Abandoned Mine*, a poetry journal

Copyright © 2023

All rights reserved.

Published by *Abandoned Mine*, a poetry journal.

ISBN: 979-8-218-15868-2

For the poets and readers

Contents

Introduction and Note:

Why This Book?
An Important Note on Formatting

Poems:

I

Gasoline   3
   Amy Beveridge

Ditched   4
   Sarah M. Brownsberger

The Thief   5
   Brian Daldorph

What We Need to Know   6
   Jeffrey Hantover

Literacy   7
   Paul Hostovsky

Walking the Perimeter of Balad Air Base, Iraq   8
   Farzana Marie

How to Do Anything Better   9
   Peggy Perdue

A Thankful Tale   10
   Bill Simmons

Concentric Futures   11
    Kim Stafford

In the Cave of Quiet   12
    Debbie K. Trantow

II

Be Like the Sun   15
    Jack Brown

Joseph Anthony   16
    Gregory L. (Goyo) Candela

Reduced to Nouns   19
    Amy Haddad

Unreported Migration   20
    Mary Mercier

Helen's Salt and Pepper Shaker Collection   21
    Marjorie Power

no other   22
    Sharon Rizk

The Hand of Aging Touches Some Gently   23
    Zack Rogow

High Noon on the River   24
    Lina Wong

III

Smokey
Robin-
son 1   27
  Alan Bern

Pluperfect   28
  Lauren Camp

Michigan   29
  Craig Cotter

Why My Mother Never Trusted Me   30
  Paul Fericano

The Change Cups Speak   31
  Emily Griffin

Portent   32
  Andrea Hollander

Second-hand Kimono   33
  Mary Makofske

Eclipse   34
  Corinne Wohlford Mason

Spiderweb   35
  Graham Murtaugh

I Once Met a Girl from Oregon   36
  Mark Nemeth

Event Horizons   37
  Prartho Sereno

Poem for President Buchanan 38
 Michael Waterson

A Fine Poem 40
 Paul Willis

IV

Colin Hay Earns a Standing Ovation 43
 Ace Boggess

Gabriel 44
 Brian Daldorph

Untitled 45
 Cameron Dean Gibson

Serendipity 46
 Gary Harrison

Gathering Beneath the Palm 48
 Katharyn Howd Machan

Fall Fox 49
 Bruce Morton

What I Remember and What I Don't 50
 Mark Nemeth

Wake 51
 William Orem

Riches 52
 Paulann Petersen

A Doctor Who Treats Himself
Has a Fool for a Patient   53
Michael Salcman

Only   54
Ellen Hirning Schmidt

The Mind-Melting Grand Ka-Pow!   55
Mark Walsh

Special Thanks

Author Bios

Why This Book?

We compiled this book for people who don't yet know they like poetry.

Many people today are of the belief that they don't "get" poetry, regarding a poem with almost the same trepidation they might regard, say, a complicated physics equation.

In fairness to those many people, some poems *are* dense. Or cryptic. Or full of confusing words. (Or all three.) Such poems can be intimidating. Such poems can sometimes dissuade people from reading more poetry.

That's a huge bummer, because most people's lives would be tremendously enriched by reading more poetry. Poetry can challenge us to more fully live out our ideals and inspire us to passionately pursue our dreams. Poetry can invite us into greater empathy for others. Poetry can help us laugh and help us cry. Poetry can make us feel not alone.

The good news is there are thousands of accessible, understandable, relatable poems in the world, ready to be discovered and enjoyed.

If you're someone who holds the belief that you don't really get poetry, hopefully the 43 thoughtful and engaging poems in this book (selected from the first four issues of *Abandoned Mine*) will help you reframe your relationship to poetry—and enrich your life!

Warmly,
Jasen Christensen & Robert Grant
Co-editors

An Important Note on Formatting

Due to the limitations presented by this book's dimensions and margins, with the author's permission we have rendered Gregory L. (Goyo) Candela's two-column poem as a one-column poem. In order to view the poem as the author intended it to appear, please visit our website, where you can read **"Joseph Anthony"** in a single-page, two-column PDF.

Also due to the book's dimensions and margins, the following three poems appear with line breaks the authors did not intend. They are:

"Michigan" by Craig Cotter
"A Fine Poem" by Paul Willis
"A Doctor Who Treats Himself Has a Fool for a Patient"
   by Michael Salcman

To view these three poems as the authors intended them to appear, please read them on our website—on a computer or in the landscape orientation on your phone or tablet.

Thank you.

I

Gasoline

Amy Beveridge

It has the odor of stopped motion, relative
of grease and metal, yet delicious to inhale,
fumes shimmering through the head like heat,
like speed, or the lightness speed brings,
splashing emptiness under our childhood
sleeping bags spread along the station wagon's hull,
the wood-paneled behemoth plowing through
the cold, clear starfield above, streaming
past ocotillo, saguaro, yucca on either side,
vibrating in the *whoosh*-wake of semis passing,
our mother trying to stay awake, alone, alone
in the front, two rows away from her girls
bundled like pupae and quietly watching
through the back window all that came before.

Ditched

Sarah M. Brownsberger

Older, taller, stronger, male,
He pants in his zeal
To leave me behind,
All knees and heels
As he pumps the pedals.

Lungs burning, tears oozing,
I reach a clearing and give up
And notice a Monarch
Poised on milkweed. Song
Sparrows thrill. I dart my hand

Past thorns for berries.

The Thief
Brian Daldorph

I'm sick of hearing about how *great*
my sister's life is, sick of her telling me
about how she's doing *astonishingly* well,
with her husband Chad's dental practice *going great guns*—
he'll be hiring a third dentist soon.
Steve's loving Little League and he's on debate team already,
and there's Katy on *YouTube* doing her flamenco,
twirling the marvelous dress her mother made!
"So how are *you* doing, Annette?"

What am I supposed to tell her about?
About my therapy with Dr. Johansson
who nods off while I talk?
Or my peach and passion fruit diet—
I've lost three pounds in two weeks.
Or my big promotion to Assistant Manager
at Food Market, with 5% discount too!

On the way out I steal my sister's keys—
bunch as big as a jailer's.
On my way home, I toss them in the river
and I laugh and laugh and laugh.

What We Need to Know

Jeffrey Hantover

How much do we need to know
to love the world?
The last major leaguer to hit .400
the name of the fifth Beatle
the Secretary of Commerce
last year's Best Supporting Actress
even what Sartre said to Simone
at the Deux Magots?

It is enough to know
the first sunset on Patmos
that caught you by surprise
around a white-washed corner
the smell of ocean air
floating over concrete and morning traffic
along the Embarcadero
the taste of heirloom tomatoes
sliced thick, drizzled with olive oil
the opening bars of Satchmo's "Summertime."
Your daughter's hand placed in yours
as natural as a rose opening to the sunlight.

Literacy

Paul Hostovsky

The roofer is not a good communicator.
He doesn't tell me when he's coming.
He misspells *debris* (leaving off the *s*)
on the handwritten estimate he gives me.
He does not inspire confidence.

But the roof turns out beautiful, the debris
gets cleared away, and the house
with its new chapeau never looked so
sophisticated. His sign, *Kilraine & Son Roofing,*
in a corner of my front yard like a signature,

topples in the wind. So I put it back
facing the house. He pulls up in his pickup,
shakes his head and repositions the sign
perpendicular to the house. So people
driving by can see it. Duh. And read it.

Walking the Perimeter of Balad Air Base, Iraq

Farzana Marie

For A. V.

I saw her pause in the wheat field,
wiping sweat from between her eyes
with the end of a cotton scarf,
both of us calculating the distance
between our paths, passing
in the topography of this moment
as close to each other as they ever would.

As my fatigues and her fatigue
exchanged glances,
I wished she could catch
on the barely-breeze the whisper
from my heart's outstretched hand:
I want to know you.

How to Do Anything Better
Peggy Perdue

This simple recipe was created for the hungry family—easy, fast, delicious. The secret? Start with what you've got:

2 cups boiling water
2 cups cold water
1 box gelatin mix
1 can assorted fruit

To put this meal together for the best presentation, and greatest chances of success, take advantage of all your senses:

1. See your daughter float into the kitchen and turn her face up to the stove.
2. Hear her ask what there is to eat.
3. Smell the toast from this morning's breakfast that she couldn't eat because you burned it.
4. Taste the saliva pool on your tongue as you try to answer.
5. Feel the space between your hip bones and ribs.

Finally, make it look effortless:

Tell her you're making a Jell-O fruit mold. She delights at the idea of dessert for dinner and hops down the hall to her room. She doesn't need to know until she's 20 that there was not food enough for tomorrow.

A Thankful Tale
Bill Simmons

When I was young

"The dish ran away with the spoon."

When I got older

The neighbor ran away with my wife.

I still believe

The cow jumps over the moon

And a cat can play the fiddle,

But I don't laugh

"To see such sport";

I thank him every day.

Concentric Futures

Kim Stafford

Inside my life resides a simpler life,
and inside that another, concentric
Russian dolls of happiness, each
waiting for me to show them sky,
birdsong, rain, the gifts of plain days,
until at last my innermost original
shrugs off all husks of complexity
to wake singing in this world.

In the Cave of Quiet

Debbie K. Trantow

This hunger is sweet as berries,
Sweet as sleep. Here I listen
Enclosed in the Great Mind.

The wide sky does not hold
These notes I've heard before.
This is a music shaped

By streams trickling down
A xylophone of rocks and ridges,
Some as fragile as glass.

Hearing the water's voice
Echo off cave walls
I mourn the skunk by the side of the road.

I count the steps of animals on the trail.
I see how long it takes for trees to grow tall.
I remember my feet on the earth.

There's a loneliness in meditation
In the cave of quiet
Where incomprehensible bells ring.

II

Be Like the Sun
Jack Brown

How do you know
when a plant loves you?

When the cat is jealous.

Sunlight bathes their
chlorophyll hearts in green glory.
The yellow God casts a heavenly spell
a scintillating aura
refulgent over fur and feline marrow.

We all get our share.

But when your attention
is too much with the cacti,
hummingbird friendly ajuga,
a transcendent daffodil,
or a lavender sprung spider plant,
the cat intercedes to distract
redirect your heart.

A cat knows the plant is sentient.
Knows when your heart
wanders from theirs.

Be like the sun.
Impartial. Warm.

Joseph Anthony

Gregory L. (Goyo) Candela

I am
Joseph
Anthony
Aragon
a coyote.
I speak in tongues.

I don't need
your goddamned meds.
I eat your food.
I don't swallow
preaching.

Don't
hand me
no pity.
Give me
dollars.

I sleep where I want.
I tear, to pieces, your
Albuquerque Journals
scatter them.
Sometimes, I
wipe my ass with

your news
not my news.

I nest in
your alleys
under
stolen   *No stanza break*

16

paint tarps.
I leave
cigarette butts
soda cups
and
candy wrappers.

I ain't afraid
of
the
dark
like you.

I mumble at
everybody. I
don't talk
with nobody.

I am a coyote.
I speak in tongues.
I scream at
the big moons.

Wrapped in
throw-away
clothes that
smell good

I rest
under thorn
fire
bushes—
no one
crawls
into—

I do.

Poem continues on next page

I burned down
a house
in L.A.
I did not know
my girlfriend
was home
asleep.

Reduced to Nouns

Amy Haddad

In grade school, I could conjugate verbs
slick as you please, slide from the present
to the past with ease. Even irregular verbs
were at the tip of my tongue.
I knew my *Je suis* from *J'etais*, imperfect
from the conditional until my thirties
when the tense I wanted hid from me.

I moved to the near future,
untied verbs from the tense, inserted *going to . . .*
before each infinitive, then filled in the blank—
I am going to eat, walk, play,
manager, marcher, jouer. There is conviction
speaking this way, diminished in the present
tense, absent from the past.

On our last trip to Paris, even infinitives
were too much for me.
I spoke only in nouns, propped up by desperate
charades. A bellman who understood
he was dealing with a pleading toddler
patiently watched me wave my arms
to outline the shape of a large car.
Une grande voiture.
I pointed at our suitcases, *Quatre bagages,*
proud I could still count to four.

Unreported Migration

Mary Mercier

—Flight belongs to those with nothing to carry.

Autumn's administration of the sky
requires no election. No ballot box
of any kind. No whiskey on the rocks
to face the tally. Only clouds go by
and that without decision. Birds comply
with gravity. One elegant wing unlocks
the sky's door. Through it entire flocks
will soar. No longer do I question why
but I do consider when. Mountains burn.
A choir sings in the dark. Nothing can stem
the rising flood of night yet birds discern
a way—following star, horizon's hem,
they leave no contrail but a brief nocturne.
One day not yet written I'll leave with them.

Helen's Salt and Pepper Shaker Collection

Marjorie Power

The display case filled
the year her son finished school
but each pair of shakers
stays perky and cute.

Her terrier sighs
on a folded blanket
near the wall with the TV.

Onscreen, a man leaves his wife
for his flame, whose husband
might die in this time slot
tomorrow or Thursday.

The story persists till Helen's hairdo
comes back into style.
She's a hottie! Always was.

no other

Sharon Rizk

back then, a young woman learned from Bedouins
in the Sahara: there are no strangers,
only degrees of difference.

anyone who passed their tent
was uncle, brother, auntie, sister.
each invited in to sweet tea, lebni, pita, dates.

now she travels up and down a gravel mountain road
to and from a cabin in New Mexico, close by Colorado.
the lesson, bone-embedded, anchored, informs choice.

when she encounters someone stopped upon that road,
especially in the snow times, she will always pause,
shift to neutral, no matter what, and ask, "You OK?"

The Hand of Aging Touches Some Gently

Zack Rogow

The hand of aging touches some gently,
lovingly smoothing cheekbones,
forehead rotundas,
and the ogives of eyes.

For others, the hand of aging
sucker punches them in the gut.
Use all the oxygen creams
and hair balayage you want:

sometimes genes just have their way.
The men on my father's side
inherit knees that give out after sixty
like branches overstocked with snow.

Seconds, minutes, hours, days:
clocks have the hungriest jaws.
Days, weeks, months, years:
life has no clickable Pause.

High Noon on the River

Lina Wong

High noon on the river came a red canoe
Gliding through the pads of water lilies,
Sun glinting off her bronze and golden hair.
She deftly slashed the over-growing vines
With a Hori-Hori her husband gifted her.

Along the bend at Cooper's Notch a man
Turned up, standing on the bank.
"What brings you here?" he queried. She was silent.
"Do you do theater?" he abruptly asked,
"I'm scouting for the remake of the old High Noon.
You could be Kane's former lover. Your hair
Is perfect for the role." And, with that,
He stepped in to the red canoe and
Deeply pierced in to her eyes with his.
His big white hands went up to stroke her hair.

She froze . . . the Hori still in hand
Upturned. She knew her stuff. With aplomb
She plunged it through his far-left side,
Avoiding major organs. Then, in one
Smooth move she pushed him overboard.
The knife, it stayed with her. The sun had moved
And dazzled off the hilt in crimson-silver.
She called, "High time you left the river," while
She paddled off, lilies in her wake.
Happy-go-lucky she was, a capable woman.

III

This is a poem that especially begs to be read aloud:

Smokey Robin- son 1
Alan Bern

Around
I shopped
She did
Too shop

We paid
And bought
The same
Good gots

Our selves
Did I
Mention
The shelves

So full
Just filled
Up stuff
Fine sale

Bowed down
Both we
Hands held
And strolled

Pluperfect

Lauren Camp

The marble teahouse has four pillars and is open on one side.
Nests in two corners. I want nothing today
but to watch two robins fly to another brisk greenery
and return to their little baskets in a current of dialects.
The irises are starting to rise and will soon be
broken-hearted. I turn the knob of my binoculars.
Sit for hours, seeing. I try on a story.
How I desire to recite the world.
A heavy mower has been grinding along and gets closer
in its gesture, summarizing a clearing.
It circulates its hungry motions, picks clean.
Silence forgives it. Through the lens I see the baby robins
hold their mouths open. Small gasping vessels.

Michigan
Craig Cotter

We weren't allowed outside until the dew dried.

I tried to explain if we played until the grass dried
wet grass would never make it into the house.

Unfortunately, at age 8, I could not make this argument
   clearly.

   —for Davin Malasarn

Why My Mother Never Trusted Me
Paul Fericano

When I could still speak to her
Without pretending I was in a vaudeville act
When she could still attempt to hear me
Without threatening to call the police

When it still made some kind of sense
To keep looking for each other in the same room

I sat with my mother at the kitchen table
Watching her light one Salem after another
Like warning flares on an unfamiliar road
And I asked her about the Great Depression

What was it like growing up
What was it like as a little girl
What was it like to be the baby in the family
Where older brothers ran away from home
To keep from starving

Did you play with dolls?
Did you ride on your father's shoulders?
Did you watch the street from your bedroom window?
Did you pray for miracles?
Did you know you had nothing?

My mother just pulled harder on her menthol cigarette
A nicotine cloud in the corner of one eye
And exhaled the dry harsh words in sweet smoky swirls
Is this another poem about me?

So much to sit with here:

The Change Cups Speak
Emily Griffin

Anybody got a light in their eyes? / Anybody on this train experienced true wonder? / Any of you able to smile a sunny hello, not the sad story of suntan leaving skin? / Does anyone really think this is fair? / Do you ever thank the wounded world for holding us? / Would you take one of my fears from me if you could? / Would you learn to replace bullets with the fog of water glasses untouched? / Who can become the radical magician that we need? / Will you vent your spleen with me? / Can we spill our indignation onto all the billionaires? / Will you show me a picture of your child looking at the world spark eyed, little amphibian smile beaming? / Can you tell me the story of that child's first steps like planting a tree, not a flag? / Can anyone put the animal grace back into the folds of their work clothes? / These creatures all depend on you being exhausted at the end of the day, you know? / Can you stomach that the little girl in the photograph will know one day, too? / How long do we have to chant our humanity to deaf ears? / How long until we all believe that there is no shame in going hungry, only in complacency about millions starving? / Do any of you have something to set free? / Does anyone remember a time before we were so greedy / and stupid / and mean? / Can anyone remember that we were once more scared of the ocean than of each other?

Portent

Andrea Hollander

He walks back into the house
later than yesterday, Daylight
Saving Time having given him
an extra hour of light, he says
when she asks. He removes his boots
in the entry, clears his throat.
The door still won't latch
and she hears him fiddling with it

again, muttering as he did
yesterday, the same few phrases
she assumes to mean he intends
to make it right tomorrow.
She's at the kitchen sink
Brillo-ing another burnt streak
she caused in one of the pans,
one more of her small blunders

that have accumulated
exponentially these last months
since he gave his word
he ended what he swore
that woman started.
This is who they were then:
the two of them trying hard
to convince themselves

that the past was the past
and not a harbinger.

Second-hand Kimono
Mary Makofske

Not silk, but cotton worn soft
by caress of breast, back, shoulder,
the hands of lovers

loose, beltless, flying open,
its winged sleeves dangerous
near kitchen flames

kindling other flames
lit by perfume, scent of bodies, sweat
the ghosts of other lives

not rich, but the everyday robe
of a woman of simple desires—
a garden, a walk at dusk

a nap at midday, blinds drawn,
her husband beside her, kimono
slipping to the floor

Eclipse

Corinne Wohlford Mason

Sometimes I have called things love
that were not love. Sometimes I have made
meaning where there was just weather or chance.

Often, my imagination too keen,
the pale face of the real thing
disappoints. This August day was
predicted long ago.

But totality, when the cicadas sang
and the shadows became
crescent, caught us
unprepared: *look at that*, said everyone
to everyone else.

The 360-degree sunset—we couldn't say how
the light had changed, only that it had.

Folks cheered and cried, as if all
our hearts had wanted, ever, were slivers of
moon scattered on concrete and grass, and nothing—

nothing more.

Spiderweb
Graham Murtaugh

Thin as old fishing line
and twice as tough,
this empty web
caught in low branches
nets a constellation
of rain-made stars,
unnoticed
but for intuition's tickle
lifting my eyes
to witness the impossible
filaments weaving
a firmament of light.

I Once Met a Girl from Oregon

Mark Nemeth

"Timber,"
she said, and I turned northwest.
"Eugene,"
and I wanted mist and drizzle,
wetsuit surfing and walks among the pines.
"Your land is a barren waste,"
and I drove circles around the mesas,
stopped and searched the night sky
for trembling stars.

Should I seek earthquakes on the Pacific Rim,
wear the famous wool and spend Halloween
in a berry patch, looking for nickel-deposit cans?
I know the grass grows greener along
the banks of the Willamette, and she says
the rain falls like moonlight or August meteors.

But aren't there deserts in Oregon, too,
where the Snake and Columbia never flow,
and even the beer bottles get dusty?

A single tree in a desert is still green, and
empty arroyos flood every July with fat,
cold drops that paint the ristras and geraniums
brighter red. The Rio Grande flows to the sea
as surely as the Columbia, past mesas
and alfalfa fields, pueblos and radio telescopes,
drawing suddenly every spring the pale green
from the brown bosque, which even in winter
is full of sandhill cranes and white snow geese.

Event Horizons

Prartho Sereno

A man now, my grandson has moved in downstairs
where he wrestles with the angels of amazement
and doubt. Our shadows bow to one another
as he leaves to drive people to the airport or city jobs.
I want to tell him things, but the guardians of predawn
won't let a whisper pass at this hour and I'm asleep

again before he comes home. I want to tell him
things, but the words have gotten snagged
in the brain's frayed cogs. The name,
for example, for the lightness
that can blow through a heart and lift it
from the body, sail it around the world.

I want to tell him, too, how the Unexpected
has a thing for us, how she hides among the pots
and pans, in wait for our little lives to whistle by.
And how nobody ever believes they are old.
One day you and your little-old-lady sweetheart
will make jokes about your slipping disguises
over scrambled eggs and toast.

Poem for President Buchanan

Michael Waterson

Your massive granite gravestone stands
in weighty contrast to your wispy legacy,
Old Buck. My home state's solitary president,
you lie forgotten, dear to none. No wonder.

Under the gun to save the Union,
you shunned a second term
at your inauguration, a startled hart,
bounding away in the woods.

After your fiancée died—
a whispered suicide—
you vowed to remain unwed,
served your four years stag.

Scholars rate it a quadrennial farce.
Proclaiming slavery evil but enshrined,
secession illegal, but ... oh, well,
you had Congress rolling in the aisles.

Shackled to you by a common bond,
our Commonwealth, I'm ashamed
you shrugged off duty, treated the office
like a trophy you'd bagged.

Before the cannons opened fire,
you hightailed it back to Pennsylvania,
penned a biography no one read,
awaited vindication.

You're waiting still, under
your unadorned ponderous monument,
gathering dust in history's basement,
down the road from Gettysburg.

A Fine Poem
Paul Willis

found by the college baseball field

Schmidt—for flipping Jones off in the chop, 25¢

Mullen—for walking across the prepped infield, 25¢

Clark—forty minutes late to practice after class, 50¢

Nogales—for leaving his glove, 75¢

Mullen—for missing second, $1.00

Jones—for hook-ups in Isla Vista, $1.00

Beauregard—for hopping the fence in cleats on a tarp,
      $1.00 for each hop

Mullen—for not knowing it was Tuesday, 25¢

Wallace—for getting yelled at by a person on a golf cart, 25¢

Murphy—for not sliding into second base, 50¢

Stefani—for sliding cleats-up into Murphy, 25¢

Wu—for taking a drink that was meant for a golf tourney
      during the 18-inning game, 50¢

Lokey—for pulling the roller with a rake and looking stupid,
      25¢

Hammond—for saying his most attractive quality was his
      nipple hair, 50¢

IV

Colin Hay Earns a Standing Ovation

Ace Boggess

—Mountain Stage, 8/22/21

We sit motionless most of the show,
austere as mannequins, masked
against the Delta variant,
our bodies props placed in seats to resemble a crowd.

"It's hard to sing & be sad at the same time,"
host Kathy Mattea says,
referring to another artist's recent death
while describing the inner sense of us.

How do we balance happiness & misery
if fear keeps its thumb on the scale?
When last folk singers leave the stage &
Colin Hay comes on, he speaks with joy

about his life, performs in a way
that infuses us with lightness.
Solo songs, covers recorded during the pandemic,
a Men at Work classic from the 80s,

something new from a record
that we must survive the year to hear—
he has us standing, uncommon
in this theater during calmer times.

We need this as much as air,
though air has never left us giddy
as if laced with laughing gas
we breathe & breathe & breathe.

Gabriel
Brian Daldorph

Gabriel slips into my room:
I can't keep him out all the time.
No locks on our doors in this place.
He sits in the chair in front of me, holds my hands,
"They're trying to kill me,
trying to poison me, they've been putting cyanide in my food
but I'm smarter than they think—I *pretend* to eat it."

Last week Gabriel warned us
of a tsunami that would sweep
us all away. "We're in the center of a continent," we said.

He's told us about missile launches
and the government counting down.
About a massive earthquake about to split
this country right down the middle.
Gabriel asks if he can have my crackers
because he's *so* hungry.

That's the trouble
that comes when everyone's trying to kill you:
it makes you so hungry.

Untitled
Cameron Dean Gibson

Thanksgiving was always a lake day,
even this year,

where all we did was sip
Michter's from the bottle

and pass the problem
of Dad

back and forth
until empty,

until we both felt
responsible enough to go home.

Serendipity

Gary Harrison

—for Marlys

bluish-grey clouds
  heavy strands
    of stratocumulus
      backlit with white
        streaks of sunlight
      press down just above
        Rio Grande Valley

translucent curtains
  of intermittent rain
    sweep over the roadway
      and thirsty carpet
        of dried grasses
      mottled with junipers
        and rabbitbrush

we woke to snowfall
  early this morning
    a low-hanging fog
      hiding the mountain ridge
        below Taos Ski Valley
      where wet snow clung
        to bare cottonwoods

where we embraced
  inside the casita
    as warm yellow light
      from the corner fireplace
        snaked along the vigas
      and stirred the earthy scent
        of stream water

with fresh memories
   of Rio Grande canyon
      the steep cliffs
         piñon and sagebrush
            stacks of broken basalt
         boulders polished black
            by the river

where two Canada geese
   wary but unafraid
      took turns bobbing
         their tuxedoed heads
            in a deep eddy
         beside the white rapids
            rushing below us

what serendipity
   in this wind-blown
      water-worn canyon
         on our anniversary day
            to meet this pair
         working and playing together
            like us, for life

47

Gathering Beneath the Palm

Katharyn Howd Machan

The women whisper, at first,
then in their checked and paisley dresses
talk more loudly because their men
are *not* around, are *not* about,
are probably shooting alligators,
delayed in demanding the brimming baskets
the women have filled with muffins and meat.
Good women, tender women, loving
life in a sun-full world with homes
they can manage for daughters and sons
still young enough to care that Mama
might cry sometimes, but it's all right.
June noon, a blue sky high
with thin black birds seeking prey.
The women share their precious time
with smiles and nods, their knowledge sure
that they will always have each other—
if not for all of life, at least
the memories of how their words
shaped into joy this one slow day.

Fall Fox

Bruce Morton

Red Reynard
He has come to visit.
Sits so still on the deck
In his fashion, full-furred,
Wearing the winter coat,
Head cocked just so, watches
Us watching him watching
Us. It is a watchoff.
Then he moves on, quiet,
To the neighbors who have
The chickens.

What I Remember and What I Don't

Mark Nemeth

I was eight.
After church, we drove to someone's house—
maybe his name was Harvey—on dusty,
pale dirt roads, halfway out to Inyokern.
I have no idea why.
We parked on a gravel driveway
next to a creosote bush.
The house faced north.
Harvey, or whoever,
was watching football, which my parents rarely did.
There were green couches, covered with clear vinyl.
No memory of Mrs. Harvey, but she was there.
Maybe we ate some cookies.
The football game was in overtime.
John Jefferson caught a long pass
two yards short of the goal line,
fell to the ground, untouched,
and rolled into the end zone.
The Chargers beat the Raiders.

Wake

William Orem

Sometimes I wake in the submarine light
and the cool stranger's house
      of early morning
and get up to pee

or detach the troublesome tabby

and, afterward, returning
to tousled sheets
in the middle of soft, first consciousness
I can't remember what on earth there is to worry about.

The hurts from decades past are not yet shaken
    from their cages;
grains of dawn rest on the banister.

What will be so avidly obvious to day—

all the detailed histories of shame and disappointment,
betrayals, faltered love—
are tightly sleeping, the Furies'
wings all tented; and I see
just for a minute

      my actual life happening:

        one human person

        standing
        in a house

as if waiting for the quietness to tell him something.

Riches

Paulann Petersen

May I learn to be poor
like a mole snubbing
the sun's largesse,
relying instead
on earth's deep pockets,

                or poor like the rain
with nothing to spend
but itself, not a blessed thing
to do but parcel itself out
into the smallest denominations
it can manage,

              or the scent
roused by that rain,
rising from a forest floor's
bottom line,

    or those mundane stones
given—by virtue of being
in a river's bed—
the gleam of wealth.

    Let me be the meadowlark,
          my throat
spent for song.

A Doctor Who Treats Himself
Has a Fool for a Patient

Michael Salcman

The first night alone, I re-warmed my wife's meatloaf and
    made rice
with cinnamon on top; the next dinner a roast beef sandwich
    with chips.
All week I ate out with friends: fried chicken, spare ribs, duck
    confit—
not a single meal with anything from the ocean except for
    oysters.
Neighbors who knew better fed me cube steak and home-
    fried potatoes.

I'd spent the month before leaking from my rectum and
    worrying over
a villous adenoma of the bowel or paralysis of my anal
    sphincter.
A day after my wife and daughter left, I didn't even fart as
    much as the cat!
I thought it must be my nightly martini or pizza, or probably
    stress,
too much tuna or purified water. As a test I stopped doing
    anything healthy

or politically correct. When the hips started hurting and my
    left leg went numb
down to the toes, I was certain my spine had narrowed at
    sixty or else
I had pissed a disc into my tail bone. Four days later all
    symptoms had gone
when I heard my wife at the door shouting "Honey, we're
    home."

Only
Ellen Hirning Schmidt

You were the only one,

he told her.

Randy, blond, blue-eyed

crush of all the girls

in Mrs. Addis' fifth grade,

playing spin the bottle

at Lynn McPhail's birthday party,

dashing in his Boy Scout uniform.

Randy's dad at the annual Firemen's Carnival

selling chance tickets.

Randy's dad called out one night,

Randy going along in the big red engine,

watching flames engulf the Jensens' house,

watching his dad step on that live wire.

At the 50th high school reunion,

he told her.

You wrote a letter to me then

to say how sorry,

he said,

You were the only one.

The Mind-Melting Grand Ka-Pow!
Mark Walsh

Too many days
too many years
I've wasted waiting
for the mind-melting grand

        Ka-Pow!

the thunder jolt that awakens
forgotten consciousness.
Waiting—
to be bowled over by beauty,
struck dumb by sound,
enfolded in Enlightenment—
forty-five years of…wait…is this it?

In truth, the mind-melting grand

        Ka-Pow!

was always available
sitting beside me,
exploding in my unhearing ears
by not exploding at all.
It reveals itself in delicate glimpses,
ekes out in small doses,
lies there in sunlight,
asking for nothing but a direct look.

The marvelous comes in minutes
moment to moment,
continually uncovered by
a single act
of paying attention.

(*Ka-Pow.*)

Special Thanks

Many people, many of them poets, played an integral role in inspiring, encouraging, and supporting us in this endeavor of starting a poetry journal. We are grateful to them all.

One in particular we feel compelled to mention by name: Paulann Petersen. She was with us at the outset with wise counsel, she contributed three wonderful poems to the journal throughout our inaugural year, and she has been with us in recent weeks providing valuable insight and feedback with regard to this our inaugural print anthology. Thank you, thank you, thank you, Paulann.

Thanks, too, to Peggy Perdue for her kind offer to help proofread early drafts of this manuscript; her attentive eye was as important as it is appreciated.

Much gratitude also to Elise Christensen, Hudson Grant, and Michael Johnson for their instincts and assistance with the final cover design. Others, too numerous to mention, also offered valuable and appreciated feedback on the cover design—and title—along the way.

This book was made possible in part by a generous donation from Pat Tipton. Abundant thanks.

Author Bios

Retired children's librarian **Alan Bern** has a hybrid fictionalized memoir forthcoming from UnCollected Press, is the author of three books of poetry, and is cofounder with artist/printer Robert Woods of fine press/publisher *Lines & Faces*. Recent awards include: Winner, Saw Palm Poetry Contest (2022); Honorable Mention, Littoral Press Poetry Prize (2021); Flash Fiction Finalist, Ekphrastic Sex (2021). Recent and upcoming writing and photo work appearing in: Haunted Waters Press, *swifts & slows*, *The Woolf*, *Mercurius*, *CERASUS*, *Feral*, and *The Hyacinth Review*. Alan performs with dancer/choreographer Lucinda Weaver as *PACES* and with musicians from Composing Together.

Amy Beveridge is a pediatric speech-language pathologist and graduate student in rhetoric and writing in Albuquerque, New Mexico. Her work has been published in *Heron Tree* and *bosque*.

Ace Boggess is the author of six books of poetry, including *Escape Envy* (Brick Road Poetry Press, 2021), *I Have Lost the Art of Dreaming It So*, and *The Prisoners*. His writing has appeared in *Michigan Quarterly Review*, *Notre Dame Review*, *Harvard Review*, *Mid-American Review*, and other journals. An ex-con, he lives in Charleston, West Virginia, where he writes and tries to stay out of trouble.

Jack Brown lives and works in New York City. Poetry published in *Adelaide*, *Aberration Labyrinth*, *The Village Sun*, *Hellcoal Annual*, and *Poets Reading the News*. He is a songwriter.

Sarah M. Brownsberger is a poet, essayist, and Icelandic-English translator. Her poems have appeared in *Salamander*, *Poetry East*, *The Hudson Review*, *Alaska Quarterly Review*, *Field*, and many other journals.

Lauren Camp is the Poet Laureate of New Mexico and author of five books, most recently *Took House* (Tupelo Press). Two new books—*Worn Smooth Between Devourings* (NYQ Books) and *An Eye in Each Square* (River River Books)—are forthcoming in 2023. Her honors include a Dorset Prize and finalist citations for the Arab American Book Award and Adrienne Rich Award for Poetry. She is a senior fellow for Black Earth Institute and was Astronomer in Residence at Grand Canyon National Park in 2022.

Gregory L. (Goyo) Candela, a professor emeritus at University of New Mexico, has resided in New Mexico since 1972. Recent publications include poems in *Adobe Walls*, *Malpais Review, Italian Americana, Circe's Lament,* and *Weaving the Terrain*. In addition, he has authored six produced plays including *El Mozo Regresa: The Kid Returns* for KUNM's Radio Theatre. His poem "Cementerios de Nuevo Mexico" was nominated for a 2018 Pushcart Prize. A new full-length book, *High Desert*, is forthcoming.

Craig Cotter was born in 1960 in New York and has lived in California since 1986. His poems have appeared in *California Quarterly, Chiron Review, Columbia Poetry Review, Court Green, The Gay & Lesbian Review, Great Lakes Review, Hawai'i Review,* & *Tampa Review*. His fourth book of poems is *After Lunch with Frank O'Hara*.

Brian Daldorph teaches at the University of Kansas and Douglas County Jail. He has taught in England, France, Japan, Senegal, and Zambia. He edits *Coal City Review* and also edited *Douglas County Jail Blues* (2010), an anthology of inmate poetry. His latest books are *Kansas Poems* (Meadowlark Press, 2021) and *Words Is a Powerful Thing* (University of Kansas Press, 2021).

Paul Fericano is a poet, satirist, social activist, and clergy abuse survivor. He is the editor and co-founder of the parody news syndicate, Yossarian Universal News Service, est. 1980. His book of poems, *Things That Go Trump in the Night* (Poem-For-All Press, 2019), was awarded the Bulitzer Prize (2020). A Room With A Pew, his blog on the healing process, often looks for humor in the shadows.

Cameron Dean Gibson is an artist working in poetry, experimental film, and *Days of Our Lives* fan fiction. His work has appeared in *Hobart, California Quarterly*, and the International Film Festival Rotterdam. He's based in Pasadena, CA.

Emily Griffin is a librarian, poet, and food enthusiast from Brooklyn, NY, who aims to capture life's most visceral experiences using interesting, accessible language. She uses techniques from both surrealist and confessional poetry traditions. Her work has been published by *High Shelf Press, Allegory Ridge, The Closed Eye Open,* and elsewhere. She earned her BFA from Emerson College and her MLS from St. John's University.

Amy Haddad is a poet, nurse, and educator who taught in the health sciences at Creighton University where she is now a Professor Emerita. Her poetry and short stories have been published in the *American Journal of Nursing, Janus Head, Journal of Medical Humanities, Touch, Bellevue Literary Review, Pulse, Persimmon Tree, Annals of Internal Medicine, Avi Magazine, DASH, Oberon Poetry Magazine*, and the anthologies *Between the Heart Beats and Intensive Care: More Poetry and Prose by Nurses* (University of Iowa Press, Iowa City, Iowa) and *Stories of Illness and Healing: Women Write Their Bodies* (Kent State University Press, Kent, Ohio). She is the 2019 recipient of the Annals of Internal Medicine poetry prize for "Families Like This" for the best poem published in the journal. She won third-place for the 2019 Kalanithi Writing Awards from

Stanford University for her poem "Dark Rides." Her first chapbook, *The Geography of Kitchens*, was published by Finishing Line Press in August, 2021. Her first poetry collection, *An Otherwise Healthy Woman*, was published by Backwaters Press, an imprint of the University of Nebraska Press, in March, 2022.

Jeffrey Hantover is a writer living in New York. His novels, *The Three Deaths of Giovanni Fumiani* (Cuidono Press) and *The Forenoon Bride* (Severn House) are forthcoming in 2023.

Gary Harrison, a retired professor of English at the University of New Mexico, has published books and articles on nineteenth-century poetry, literature and ecology, and world literature. His recent poems have appeared in *A Wind Blows Through Us* and in *Abandoned Mine*. Since his retirement, Gary has focused his energies on writing poetry, hiking and backpacking, and composing songs. He is working on a collection of poems—"trailogues"—recording impressions of nature at home and in the deserts, canyons, and mountains of Arizona, Colorado, New Mexico, and Utah.

Andrea Hollander moved to Portland, Oregon, in 2011, after living for more than three decades in the Arkansas Ozarks, where she was innkeeper of a bed & breakfast for 15 years and Writer-in-Residence at Lyon College for 22. Hollander's fifth full-length poetry collection was a finalist for the Best Book Award in Poetry from the American Book Fest; her fourth was a finalist for the Oregon Book Award; her first won the Nicholas Roerich Poetry Prize. Her poems and essays appear widely in anthologies, college textbooks, and literary journals, including a recent feature in *The New York Times Magazine*. Other honors include two Pushcart Prizes (in poetry and literary nonfiction) and two fellowships in poetry from the National Endowment for the Arts. In 2017, she initiated the Ambassador Writing Seminars, which she conducted in her home, but via Zoom since the pandemic.

Paul Hostovsky's latest book of poems is *Mostly* (FutureCycle Press, 2021). His poems have won a Pushcart Prize, two Best of the Net Awards, and have been featured on Poetry Daily, Verse Daily, and *The Writer's Almanac*.

Katharyn Howd Machan, a longtime professor in the Department of Writing at Ithaca College, has served as coordinator of the Ithaca Community Poets and director of the Feminist Women's Writing Workshops, Inc. Her poems have appeared in numerous magazines, anthologies, textbooks, and collections (most recently *Dark Side of the Spoon* from The Moonstone Press in 2022 and *A Slow Bottle of Wine*, winner of the Jessie Bryce Niles Chapbook Competition, from Comstock Writers, Inc. in 2020), and she has edited three thematic works, including *Adrienne Rich: A Tribute Anthology* with Split Oak Press. For body and spirit, she belly dances.

Mary Makofske's latest books are *The Gambler's Daughter* (chapbook, The Orchard Street Press, 2022), *World Enough, and Time* (Kelsay, 2017) and *Traction* (Ashland Poetry, 2011), winner of the 2010 Richard Snyder Award. Her poems have appeared in *Poetry East, The American Journal of Poetry, Southern Poetry Review, Spillway, Talking River Review, Valparaiso Poetry Review*, and other journals and in nineteen anthologies.

Farzana Marie lives in Albuquerque, New Mexico, and has lived in Afghanistan, Kazakhstan, Chile, California, and Arizona. She is a poet with a Ph.D. from the University of Arizona (focus: Persian Literature, with a minor in Creative Writing). Farzana's captivating poetry and translations have appeared in print and online journals *(Flycatcher, Atticus Review, Zócalo, Blue Streak,* etc.*)*. Farzana honorably served in the U.S.

Air Force, including back-to-back deployments in Afghanistan where she also served as a civilian volunteer at a Kabul orphanage in 2003-2004. She has written a collection of Persian Dari poetry in translation *(Load Poems Like Guns)*, a poetry chapbook *(Letters to War and Lethe)*, and a nonfiction book *(Hearts for Sale! A Buyer's Guide to Winning in Afghanistan)*.

In 2015, in Kabul, Afghanistan, Farzana had a massive stroke. Today she is facing a new adversary: aphasia—a loss of language skills (not intellect). Now she is working every day to recover her ability to speak, read, and write.

Corinne Wohlford Mason teaches US history, culture studies, and writing at Fontbonne University in St. Louis, where she also chairs the Department of Humanities. She holds an MFA in poetry from Washington University and a PhD in American studies from St. Louis University. Her poems have been published or are forthcoming in *Phoebe*, *Hawai'i Pacific Review*, *Harvard Review*, *New Ohio Review*, *Southern Indiana Review*, *Pleaides*, the *Grolier Poetry Prize* annual, and elsewhere. She was nominated for a Pushcart Prize in 2022.

Mary Mercier is a poet inspired by nature, flight, and the barking of crows. Her poems have been published in *Blueline*, *Common Ground Review*, *Stoneboat*, *The Comstock Review*, and other journals.

Bruce Morton splits his time between Montana and Arizona. He was formerly a librarian at Montana State University.

Graham Murtaugh is a licensed mental health counselor and unlicensed poet writing from the ancestral lands of the Puyallup people in what is now Tacoma, WA. He has published in several journals and released one chapbook, *There Is No Safety* (Self-Titled Press, 2013).

Mark Nemeth holds a Ph.D. in civil engineering and works as an engineer for a federal water management agency. His research has been published in the *Journal of Hydrology* and the *International Journal of River Basin Management*. He lives in Albuquerque, New Mexico.

William Orem's first collection of stories, *Zombi, You My Love*, won the GLCA New Writers Award, formerly given to Louise Erdrich, Sherman Alexie, Richard Ford, and Alice Munro. His second collection, *Across the River*, won the Texas Review Novella Prize. His first novel, *Killer of Crying Deer*, won the Eric Hoffer Award and has been optioned for film. His first collection of poems, *Our Purpose in Speaking*, won the Wheelbarrow Books Poetry Prize and was published by MSU Press. It also won the Rubery International Book Award in poetry and was chosen Book of the Year. His second novel, *Miss Lucy*, won the Gival Press Novel Award, and Kirkus listed it as one of the Best Books of 2019. He has been nominated for the Pushcart Prize five times, in poetry, fiction, and creative nonfiction.

Also, his short plays have been performed internationally, winning both the Critics' Prize and Audience Favorite Award at Durango Theatre Fest, and thrice being nominated for the prestigious Heideman Award at Actors Theatre of Louisville.

William is currently a Senior Writer-in-Residence at Emerson College.

Peggy Perdue was a 2017/18 Atheneum Fellow at the Attic Institute of Arts and Letters. She lives in her own world, where she spends most of her time thinking, imagines everything is waaayyy easier than we're making it, and refuses to wake up early. She is currently putting the final touches on her first chapbook.

Paulann Petersen, Oregon Poet Laureate Emerita, has seven full-length books of poetry, most recently *One Small Sun*, from Salmon Poetry in Ireland. *My Kindred*—an eighth collection that includes her poem "Riches"—is forthcoming from Salmon Poetry. A Stegner Fellow at Stanford University, she received the 2006 Holbrook Award from Oregon Literary Arts. In 2013 she was Willamette Writer's Distinguished Northwest Writer. In 2022, the Latvian composer Eriks Esenvalds commissioned three poems from her to use as the lyrics in his new three-part choral composition, *Naming the Rain*.

Marjorie Power's newest full-length poetry collection is *Sufficient Emptiness* (Deerbrook Editions, 2021). A chapbook, *Refuses to Suffocate*, appeared from Blue Lyra Press in 2019. *Atlanta Review*, *Barrow Street*, *Mudfish*, *Southern Poetry Review*, *DASH*, *The RavensPerch*, and *EPOCH* have taken her work recently.

Sharon Rizk received a BA in English Literature and returned to school as an older adult to earn an MS and PsyD in Clinical Psychology. She resides in an LGBTQ community near Santa Fe, NM, where she has a small clinical practice. She is a published poet and has been nominated for a Pushcart. An audio CD of selected poems, *The Shadow of Your Longing: Poems to Grow With*, was released in 2010.

Zack Rogow is the author, editor, or translator of more than twenty books or plays. His ninth book of poems, *Irreverent Litanies*, was published by Regal House. He is also writing a series of plays about authors. The most recent of these, *Colette Uncensored*, had its first staged reading at the Kennedy Center in Washington, DC, and ran at the Canal Cafe Theatre in London, as well as in San Francisco and Portland. He serves as a contributing editor of *Catamaran Literary Reader*.

Michael Salcman, poet, physician, and art historian, was chairman of neurosurgery at the University of Maryland and president of the Contemporary Museum. Poems appear in *Arts & Letters*, *The Café Review*, *Hopkins Review*, *The Hudson Review*, *New Letters*, and *Poet Lore*. Books include *The Clock Made of Confetti*, *The Enemy of Good Is Better*, *Poetry in Medicine* (his popular anthology of classic and contemporary poems on doctors, patients, illness, and healing), *A Prague Spring, Before & After* (winner of the Sinclair Poetry Prize), and *Shades & Graces* (the inaugural winner of The Daniel Hoffman Legacy Book Prize, published by Spuyten Duyvil in 2020). *Necessary Speech: New & Selected Poems*, also from Spuyten Duyvil, appeared in early 2022.

Ellen Hirning Schmidt first submitted poems for publication when she turned 70 in 2017. She has received the Helen Kay Chapbook Prize, a Pushcart nomination, and a Connecticut Poetry Society Award. Her poems have appeared widely. Her chapbook, *Oh, Say Did You Know*, is available from Evening Street Press. Her first full-length collection of poems, *Armed to the Teeth*, is scheduled for publication by Antrim House Books in 2023.

After retiring from a crisis center, Schmidt designed Writing Through the Rough Spots, a class enabling students to create clarity about life challenges through writing. Her students, teens-80s, have come from across the U.S. and 15 countries. She leads workshops online and at Star Island, NH. A mother and grandmother, Schmidt lives with her husband in Ithaca, NY.

Prartho Sereno is the author of four prize-winning poetry collections, including, most recently, *Indian Rope Trick* (Blue Light Book Award, 2018), and her illustrated *Causing a Stir: The Secret Lives & Loves of Kitchen Utensils*. Poet Laureate Emerita of Marin County, CA, she taught poem-making to children in grades K through 12 as a California Poet in the

Schools for over 21 years, and she currently teaches "The Poetic Pilgrimage: Poem-Making as Spiritual Practice" online.

Bill Simmons, B.A. in English/Philosophy from Fresno State, focus on reading and writing poetry. Mentors: Peter Everwine, C. G. Hanzlicek, and Philip Levine. Lived in Carroll, Iowa, for 20 years, read at local colleges, DMACC, and started a writing group with the instructors and conducted a writing group at the local library. Now lives in Fresno, California, and is starting another poetry group.

Kim Stafford is the founding director of the Northwest Writing Institute at Lewis & Clark College, and author of *The Muses Among Us* and *Singer Come from Afar*. He served as Oregon's Poet Laureate from 2018-2020, and has taught writing in Mexico, Scotland, Italy, and Bhutan.

Debbie K. Trantow holds an MFA in Creative and Professional Writing from the University of Minnesota, where she won the 2001 Gesell Summer Writing Fellowship. Her chapbook *Hearing Turtle's Words* was published by Spoon River Poetry Press. In addition, she's been published in *Gertrude*, *The North Coast Review*, *The Wisconsin Review*, *Gyroscope*, *Poem*, and other literary magazines and journals.

Mark Walsh is an English professor at Massasoit Community College in Brockton, MA, where he teaches literature and philosophy. Through Massasoit Television, he created *Writers at Work*, and is developing a new show, *Out of the Marvelous*, focusing on poets and poetry in Southeastern Massachusetts. Since the mid-1990s he has helped organize and host poetry readings in Plymouth and Brockton. Recently, Mark was the head judge of the selection team for the City of Brockton's first-ever Youth Poet Laureate. He is a submissions reader for the *Lily Poetry Review*, and his journalism has appeared in *The South Shore News* & *The Marshfield Mariner*. His poetry publications include *The Beatnik*

Cowboy, Wilderness House Literary Review, and *Abandoned Mine*. Most recently, his "haiku for the second buyer" was published in *South Shore Real Producers*, a trade magazine for realtors in Massachusetts.

Michael Waterson is a retired journalist originally from Pittsburgh, PA. His career includes stints as a forest firefighter, San Francisco taxi driver, and wine educator. He earned an MFA from Mills College. His work has appeared in numerous online and print journals, including *California Quarterly*, *Cathexis Northwest*, and *The Bookends Review*. His first collection, *Cosmology of Heaven and Hell*, was published in 2022.

Paul Willis has published seven poetry collections, the most recent of which is *Somewhere to Follow* (Slant Books, 2021). Individual poems have appeared in *Poetry*, *Ascent*, *Writer's Almanac*, and the *Best American Poetry* series. He is a professor of English at Westmont College in Santa Barbara, California.

Lina Wong grew up in New Jersey on the Hudson River and now lives in Rio Rancho on the Rio Grande. She loves the skies, land, mountains, and snow of New Mexico. Her other favorite place is Mount Desert Island, Maine. When not working as a nurse, she likes to play Chopin, grow daisies and dahlias, and clamber up the La Luz Trail.

www.ingramcontent.com/pod-product-compliance
Lightning Source LLC
Chambersburg PA
CBHW020331130626
46549CB00003B/1129